HUMSANITY

**Poems
and
Illustrations
by
Michael
Victor Jackson**

**michaelmilkyway
productions**

Published in Great Britain by michaelmilkyway productions,
Bath, 2012

www.michaelmilkyway.co.uk

British Library Cataloguing in Publication Data

ISBN 978-0-9573391-0-1

Printed and bound in Great Britain by Lightning Source UK,
Milton Keynes

CONTENTS

FOREWORD

We always find comfort in that which is familiar to us no matter what stone we discover it under. Recognising patterns, being essential to the learning process, enables us to bring ideas together and form a network of associations we end up calling reality. To a new born child however, this reality must seem like a fragmented foreign world.

Although everyone's experience of life and meaning of life is unique, common ground is found between numerous groups of people that results in the establishment of a variety of communities and cultures. By mimicking each other we shape and strengthen *reality* and self-identity which, in truth, is no more or less than one of an uncountable number of possible proposals. However, familiarity isn't bias and always offers us the comfort necessary to sustain a certain quality of life.

Like the ageing process that goes unnoticed, until you take another look at a photo of yourself, which is old enough to have collected some dust, we have a natural blindness to that which we spend most of our time with. What effectively happens is, the more time we spend in a particular place or the longer we look at something, have certain thoughts, act in a certain way etc. the less aware of them we become. Such things then turn into the normality that disappears in front of our eyes. You could say the less we look at others the less we know ourselves. Have you notice when on holiday somewhere exotic that the magic you see before you, for the locals, is absolutely normal. This phenomenon I call familiarity blindness and, at some degree or another, it naturally happens regardless of the lifestyle and belief system we may support.

With that said, the more time we spend with something the more real it seems to be, the stronger our identity appears to become and the more comfort, direction and security we believe we gain from it.

We no longer have to imagine the dangers that can arise when non self-reflective unquestioning minds begin to mimic each other and duplicate throughout large societies. A certain amount of ignorance is key to preserving enough space to keep learning however, once we start overdosing on it, like the negative effect of any addiction/obsession, it loses its necessity and becomes suicidal. Because of the comfort we find in the familiar, the longer we stay uncritical, the more likely we are going to close our door to that which is unknown, foreign and new and not necessarily realise it. Ignorance is ignorant to its own ignorance. To the extent that the learning process then becomes rigid and absolute paradoxically means that both extreme ignorance and absolute knowledge result in stagnation. Ignorance has no interest in learning, and knowing everything means there is nothing else to learn. Like I have suggested, a certain amount of ignorance is required to make room for knowledge and understanding to enter, so without the duality one obliterates the other. Without wisdom there is no ignorance and vice versa.

Obsession is simply a state of having few interests, the fewer you have the more obsessed you become about them. It is perfectly understandable that someone who is obsessed with just few interests, would put up a thick wall of defence in defence of any external challenge to his beliefs. If the obsessive had only one interest, the questioner would be challenging the person's whole identity and reality. Without providing any better offer, such an attack would be an outright declaration of total war. If, on the other hand, you had a thousand different interests at your disposal, to drop a few here and there wouldn't be of any concern.

With that said, although we all need a certain amount of familiarity from which we can base opinion, learn, grow and experience consciousness, anything new, unquantifiable and foreign is first viewed with cynicism. Foreign, strange, odd, weird, peculiar, alien etc. are all well practised adjectives we use to describe that which is new. So, although getting to know the alien is necessary to rid it of its strangeness and allow us to learn, grow, and become aware, our fight or flight instinct plus our cultural influences combined treat any newcomer as a potential threat to our pseudo-identity, comfort zone and reality. So, on the one hand we have the curiosity of an explorer but, on the other hand, we are reluctant to leave our home sweet home, which we are now largely blind to. There's is a truth in the three sayings: "The more you know, the less you know", "The less you know, the more you believe you know" and "Ignorance is bliss". As every experience offers something new to learn, from a daily natter with our neighbours to experiencing the whole of life, means we are going through a permanent identity crisis. Balance is required. Throughout history the status quo has always been kept on its toes by the beauty of innovation. We are continuously sculpting and redesigning reality by the creativity naturally expressed by simply existing. Again, like the ageing process only being noticeable when looking back at a time we had mechanically frozen, the state of a situation only becomes clear when it is taken out of its familiar invisible context and put on the retrospective show. Take, for example, Marcel Duchamp's *Fountain*. A bog standard urinal, signed with the pseudonym "R. Mutt". *Fountain* was exhibited as a work of art that shocked the art world in 1917. However, once again only after the event, in the safety of the academia where dust settles, was it to be considered arguably the most influential artwork of the 20th century. How challenging proposals are, from painting your living room walls a different colour to the announcement that the world is round or the arrival of *Einstein's Theory of Relativity*, depends on how open you choose to be to the unknown.

With that said, living in a culture which is continuously having its thoughts and opinions heavily regulated by façade, nonsense and ignorance, primarily by the airbrushed pixel world of mass media, we are more likely to watch a DIY type programme on how to decorate our home sweet home in thirty minutes on prime time TV than we are to consume an in depth analysis of physics. As the glossy camouflage of quick fix fantasy fills the shelves and then our minds, we are also going to find prime time DIY shows much more intellectually stimulating and comforting than anything critical, as they affirm the very same identity we have attached ourselves to. Popularised designer wars are then manifested in the mind of the idiot culture by two dimensional rulers in order to strengthen the idea that Big Brother, the series not the reading of George Orwell's 1984, is a freedom worth dying for.

The mechanical, soldier like population, that makes up such a society ends up only feeling relaxed while in a state of sedated blindness. The only experience we then have of being alive is the irritation felt when our favourite programme has been postponed, or the shelves of the convenient store aren't over flowing, or the family photo oddly ends up being moved a centimetre away from its *rightful* place. When this happens war is declared on variety and life itself and the photograph is often quickly moved back to its usual place in order for it to be ignored for the next ten years.

Only when the foreigner becomes so present, that you can no longer ignore it tearing apart your foundations you have been blindly sleeping on, you start to question reality and find yourself in the spot light of self-reflection.

Creativity is always a foreigner
ready to invade.

Michael Victor Jackson

M.F.A.

Artist, writer, philosopher

THE POLITE

I never said please and never said thank you
Nobody seemed to ask
But now I can speak you push all the time
You are sorry for this
You are thankful for that

So now I am four and after forgiveness
For something I had never done
So thank you for these
And may I have those?
I'm sorry I played with my toes

I'll forgive you this time for you were only a child
You never knew right from wrong
But step out of line just one more time
And that will be the end of the song

So now I am ten and after forgiveness
For something I had never done
So thank you for these
And may I have those?
I'm sorry I played with my toes.

THE DARKENED MIRROR

An ocean without each drop of water is but dry land
A desert for want of a grain is less than even sand

An artist without a brush is but a mouth without a tongue
When the voice that sings the song of life
Is a breath without a lung

A wound that heals and leaves no scar
Would seem somewhat bizarre

So looks the darkened mirror
Of a universe
Without a star.

THE NUMBER THREE

A silent mind full of potential
An aimless wind that was always on target
Heading for a tree to find its tongue
Let's create a sensation there's a song to be sung

Some call me God others Krishna
I'm also a soup a primate whisper
A drunken accident put me in labour
A well planned baby made me a saviour

The duality code love versus hate
Was bound to stir an eruptive debate
The idea of progression can make me look old
Innate wisdom however, lets my story be told

Here I am everything other than you
There I am everything even a shoe
Deep in the jungle the fittest survive
High up in a tree the atheist's alive

Back in the soup I got out of bed
Stretched and washed just to be bred
Adam and Eve didn't I know
Satan would come to kick off the show?

Everyone's equal in the eyes of Lord
As I sit on my thrown hand on my sword
Giving away your responsibility
I became judge of your slavery

Wars have been fought under my name
But hey what the *hell* it's only a game
Fingers that shout they're barbaric I'm tame
Selling your choice by shifting the blame

Shame the soup didn't evolve sunglasses
That life bearing star missed by the masses
But let's not hang on to a minor regret
Head for the bookies and place a new bet

My knowledge is perfect so why would I hope
Maybe my dealer won't bring me my dope
You'd put me in jail throw away the key
Start learning French c'est la vie

Here in my cell heading for hell
Remembering the universe with my ear to a shell
But here I am at home with my most critical trainee
As I gaze in the mirror narcissistically

Your magician am I with one flick of my wand
Your potential am I to take you beyond
Your logic am I to take my last breath
Your deserter am I to put me to death

You and me in duality
The finite versus infinity
But empathy means unity
The universal number 3.

TRYING

I tried to call you but you weren't there
I tried to lose my way
I tried so hard for the sake of trying
So never went astray
I tried to laugh when the funny man asked
How much did you have to pay?
So now I lay down beside my bed
And try to die this way.

MODESTY

Never have I heard a modest bird singing to the breeze
A modest man on the other hand sings on his knees

If Mohamed Ali that bumble bee danced with half a sting
That butterfly would have been too shy to have kept him in the ring

No my friend modesty is too polite for me
I'll take my drive and stay alive to be or not to be.

TURNING UP THE SOUND

Let's grapple with the splintered wood in the rushing rapids
Throw ourselves over board full of drunken acids
The beat goes on the flag held high never touch the ground
With full beam on and boggled eyes turning up the sound

They're in our sight my hollow torch writing to the widows
My fading me like yesterdays running in the meadows
The beat goes on the flag held high never touch the ground
With full beam on and boggled eyes turning up the sound

So here we are click click click dancing for your land
And there you are Uncle Sam writing on demand
The beat goes on the flag held high never touch the ground
With full beam on my boggled eyes turning up the sound.

PARTNERS IN CRIME

To fear death is for beginners
I get a dollar every time I die
To fear death is for the sinners
So I built a castle in the sky

Life's not waiting with the door ajar
Jump right in swim with the tide
No Hollywood sequel of a distant star
Face to face no seek no hide

Hope and fear fester like a wound in a waiting room
Anticipating the worst in their world of doom and gloom
Begging that it's true that they can do so much these days
Sit around wait your turn here's a picture gaze

Hope and fear have been partners for many many years
Making golden anniversaries look like newly weds
Sitting on the fence of doubt counting all the tears
Tattooed in the shipwreck skin, snakes leave in sheds

Sleeping through the winter hope waits for the spring
Dreaming of the birds of peace how beautiful they sing
First sign of daffodils fear looking at dismay
Unknowing shrills as autumn chills and the sky turns to grey

I hope it all goes well when you meet your worst enemy
Nervous wreck unlucky me goading a world of misery
Run from fear into fear hoping pain will go away
Wave a wand count to three everything will be okay

Hope and fear are peculiar things ending when wishes are granted
Destiny out of control like a Christmas list to Santa if Claus-e
You are good like your superiors commanded
Strike lucky get your treat as you sink to forgiven flaws

Hope and fear are partners in crime swapping roles each step I take
Playing good cop bad cop split personality until I'm ready to break
Face to face with the pain make it real that's my gain
Reflecting substance, responsibility, sanity, there's no one to blame

I walk around with hungry bears
We are free no hierarchy
We undo entangled snares
We're not just some wannabe

Life and death come naturally
Not cosmetically
Not nervously
And not in a factory

My responsibility
My potentiality
My destiny
My destiny

My Des-ti-ny.

SAME AGAIN?

The doormat reads *Home Sweet Home*
Filling the cracks so we are never alone
The routines, the structures, our daily lives
Seem to give us direction among the cries

We can soon put an end to that fluttering flame
Plastic next year, my dear, that's the game
The barman will pour us a glass of our usual
That home sweet home taste of blissful delusional.

THE TRICKSTER'S SON

Good luck my son
Hold your head up high and be brave
A pint of courage will do the trickster's trickery my son

It could be quick it could be slow
But you, my son, will never know.

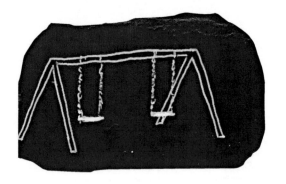

MY FOE

Before your birth my dearest son
I planned you all along
There is no yes without a no
No right without a wrong

Project myself onto you
Mission of the day
Then you will see my dearest son
Never must you stray

You'll look away and see a void
Nowhere you will go
For fear you'll have my dearest son
For there awaits my foe.

PERFECTION

Okay, no one's perfect so we're more like a dialect
Regional jargon
I beg your pardon
Lacking understanding outside Tinyland

So now we've outlawed being flawless
The thought is now crude and insane
Banished locked up and deported abroad
As if it was something profane

But look at me I am a human
Being human in every way
My way is to be at every degree
I simply can not go astray

When I get up I get up
When I fall down I fall down
But when I walk tall you tell me I'm small
And turn me perfectly into your clown

Seeing you in me is your fear
To be laughed at and ran out of town
So we'll sing our song at the end of the pier
When you realise that we are profound.

THE CAFÉ

I thought wearing rose coloured glasses was
just a figure of speech, but there's an old
worn out woman sitting right in front of me
who *is* wearing rose coloured glasses

The smell of burning fat gives this greasy
spoon café an Auschwitz flavour
Like cold tobacco smoke, the death of fat also
tends to stick and follow you home

I suppose this is one way of explaining to my
boy how history seems to repeat itself

Was there ever a gap?

Dressed up lard in suits ordered to take
orders from invisible lords
To wear wide smiles and shiny teeth
In front of a backdrop of glossy pictures of
crispy beef

In the café everyone's a touch screen killer
Now the children are screaming for flesh
while parents hold them back like you would
a wild animal pulling on its leash

We come into this joint alone and leave alone
No word or glimpse shared
among those who had once cared

But in the midst of it all, still too small to
know the meaning of being rude
A tiny voice clearly speaks
"This summer is particularly wet and with
virtually every seedling being gobbled up by
the slug army it looks like we will be in for a
hard famine come September"

Like cash in hand revolts normally kick off
under the table
but this time a sunflower has grown out of
the land fill for all to see

And the voice spoke again
"Now that's what I call being rude"
And he then lent over to show me his
spider tattoo on his arm.

HAYSTACKS

For the same reason squirrels collect and hide nuts
For those cold winter evenings
We gather dry hay
To make our bed warm and snug

Truth itself sits patiently in the corner of a room
Like a whisper in a football stadium

In response to its innate magnetism
We slowly shuffle our way
Through the cheering crowd
In search of it

As our hearing starts to adapt
To the roar of the chanting fans
We begin to forget how loud their cry is
As the bedlam turns into a whisper

It's on those warm summer days
When dry hay burns best.

SCRIBBLES ON DOTTED LINES

Scribbles on dotted lines make the world go round
Unless of course you are talking to a realist
Just put the song on you ain't nothin' but a hound
Dogs of war linger like a rash in red mist

Go to the doctor take a pill forget about the rest
Rest HA not for years cos you say I am blessed
Blessed with what kiss your feet forget about the plot?
Shed a tear have a beer if it gets too hot

Think of your family what they'd do without a dotted line
Think they'd trust you get innate and say that you're sublime?
Out of work TV on get a bunch of this
They'll look at you confused Mr. Wealthfree
asking why you take the piss

No more shooter no more movies now that would be a crime
Pictureless books words that rhyme not even worth a dime
Keep your mouth shut Mr. Poverty and fulfil the contract you are under
There's a thousand more out there who wouldn't think twice
about putting you in a slumber

This is a how world not a why world
This is a now world and a lie world
But now I ask why like we all do inside
For this is where movement will always reside

Scribbles on boggy stagnation is the Utopian no-place
Where dotted lines turn humans into Mr. & Mrs. No-face
Nature is why before it is how
It answers with movement and not with a bow

It needs no applause and makes no encore
It repeats itself not once so avoids being a bore
Dotted lines dress you up and turn you into a clown
Looking like a Christmas tree they'll say you are profound

Okay Mr. Poverty we'll put you on TV
Make you big make you real make it sound like you really feel
So when you die the world can cry
And you will fly eternally

Just sign the dotted line so you can be sublime
Decoration is probation
Just think of your family Mr. Poverty
My name is Humanity and I'm going home.

GOOD CAPTAINS HAVE GREAT NAVIGATORS

Before the waters settle the dam has to break

The flood!!!

They calm

We manifest ourselves in the form of a pulsating boil!!!

Shhh calm.

AEROPLANES

My vision of your potential is your anchor
So strong is its current it will drag you under

Until the last bubble of life leaves your burning heart
I will adore you

But the sun doesn't penetrate the thickening waters of lost time
as well as it used to

So until we finally go blind
adoration and I will watch aeroplanes fly by.

WALKING

Life is a mist impossible to anchor
Always on the move too slippery to hold
Try as we may to contain it enslave it
As if it were a product to be packaged and sold

Trying will only make us good at trying
Chasing a dream produced by the cold
Placed in the future that unreachable distance
As the potter sits at his wheel with nothing to mould

Complete are the ones who evaporate
Taking flight in warm air letting go of control
Jumping from mountains no fear of dying
Listening to the breeze sharing the stories we roll

These are the days we put dying behind us
Bringing ambition back to our home
Walking to Bath for the love of walking
Not living a life just to sit on some thrown.

THE EEL

Have you forgotten yet again that your nature is to slip?
The slippery wiggly eel you are so slip slip slip

To grasp you is to slip with you
So trash the mirror of vanity
To dry up like a prune is a higgledy-piggledy sanity

So somersault through the oceans
Be the eel without a net
To slip and slide with nature is the harmonious duet.

WHERE EVER

Where ever responsibility can be bought we're left with inability
Where ever understanding can be bought we're left with fear
Where ever ethics can be bought we're left with immorality
Where ever freedom can be bought we're left with slavery
Where ever opinion can be bought we're left with silence
Where ever love can be bought we're left with distrust
Where ever life can be bought we're left with death
Where ever we can be bought there's nothing left
Freedom = Choice
Choice = Responsibility
Responsibility = Freedom
Choice freedom and responsibility
The universal number 3.

Birth, death and tornadoes
don't say please or thank you.
So either nature is rude
or politeness decadently crooked.

Laws are based
on the economy
not on ethics.

The judges' opinion
is determined
according to the
situation he finds
himself in.

You can only be brave
if you are frightened.
People who know thing
don't tend to get med
or a hero's welcome.

Fear and hope are
anticipations and
fantasies, not
reality.

Obsession is simply
having few interests.
The fewer you have
the more obsessive
you become.

Modesty is a simple lie.
You can't be modest in
private, the motivation
isn't there.

Modesty and politeness
go out the window
when the situation
becomes desperate.

The less aware
we are the more
quick fixes we
need and
the more
obsessive we
become.

If sacrifice was
natural then nature
wouldn't have even
began.
The impossibility
of sacrifice.

The difference between fascism and modern day democracy is the packaging.

If true knowledge can not be obtained all we leave ourselves with is subjective nonsense, isolation and division.

Only where there is fear there is hope. And both end when reality kicks in.

Hope is for the nervous.

The idea of sacrifice always leads to regret blame and debt.

Where there is understanding there is nothing to fear, forgive or regret.

Normal isn't always natural. Fear and distrust have become very normal.

Familiarity is necessary but it isn't bias.

New laws make old laws illegal although old laws makers don't tend to go to prison.

Misunderstand language and we misunderstand humanity.

A responsible person encourages responsibility while an irresponsible person sells it.

Not every honest smile drowns in the swamp of distrust

That spark That reminder of togetherness.

In a society built upon insecurity, fear and contracts replace respect and trust.

McVINCI

Keep Leo quiet in the back seat
He's making jerky movements dad I think he's on heat
Wave to the camera kids smile you're on TV

Flash!!!

What 31mph
Did they see me?

GPS McVinci drive through left 700 meat-ers
Look at Lisa Mona kids when we start to eaters
Don't say that they're too young you're gonna go to jail
What me VIP permanently on bail?

Three triple triple triples one double double
Bubble bubble bubble could be some trouble
Hello can I take your order?
Oh, yes please, may I have 4 merry go rounds
And half a baker's dozen rose coloured glasses?

Sink your teeth in taste the red
WOW it's still alive
Pop pop pop full of lead now we're talking dead
CD on giving gas on Highway 35
I think we are lost, aren't we meant to be on Route 66?

Sixty six 666 thirty bucks a fix
Stop this now and let's go home.

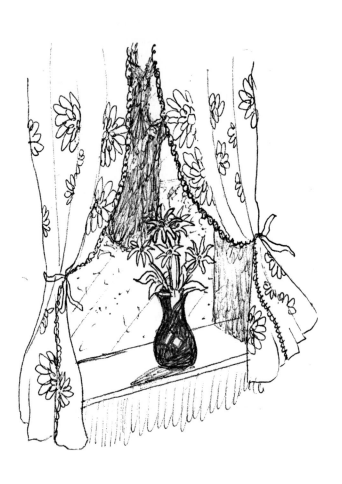

THE SEVENTH DAY

Hunger starts to grow as that yummy smell flows
Leaking from the oven on a Sunday afternoon
Close my eyes make a wish and really mean it this time
Snap goes the wishing bone

Window open wide now spring has filled the air
Celebrating life once more with that roasted festive flare
Flowers blooming bees dancing sky is full of song
It was a heavy winter we had to wait so long

Table set EastEnders on one till ten to three
Omnibus edition for the whole family to see
Crispy golden skin the leg is mine this time
Past the salt and pepper if you'd be so kind

Teeth sinking into veins tongues licking up the arteries
Turn the TV up damn birds still singing in the trees
Flesh a little tough my dear next time it should be tender
Was a baby honey frozen sell by date November

Don't give the dog all the red you know he's a little piggy
Sunday market got early stage rigor mortis babies my little schmooze
Forgot to say sweetheart Mary phoned yesterday she's had a little boy
Wow hammers robots and football rock 'n' roll and blues.

ALL ABOARD THE SCARLET EXPRESS

The whistle blows to vote in dominion
To level that meaning of all opinion
Lo and behold now the truth be told
The winters are hot and the summers are cold
You are but you I am but me
As we all embrace subjectivity.

NOVEMBER CHRISTMAS

Mid November in Clockwork Town
Once again the Christmas songs start to bellow in the background
Just below the threshold level
As if I keep coming up with the idea myself.

THE 1st MAY

My knowledge is perfect in every way
Forever and a day
All questions subside
With answers supplied
Farewell to the 1st of May

But in you I forget and this is my gain
My break from knowing the way
All questions arrive
For answers can hide
How joyful
The 1st of May

But now I am back before I could leave
For departure is the mark of my stay
All questions subside
With answers supplied
Farewell to the 1st of May.

A PINT OF I'M ACCUSTOMED

This is the way to write poetry
Providing us with that familiarity
An affirmative measure of reality
Logically fitting in comfortably

This is the way to get blind drunk my dear
Hold the class tight and sign here my dear
Don't challenge the way or sneer my dear
I've been doing this for too many years

This is the way to silence history
Build up a nation on conformity
Make us feel at home ritualistically
End of part one
Cup of tea?

So
Secure me
Deplore me
Crucify me
And
Adore me
Just give me
Familiarity.

RECLUSE SWEET RECLUSE

From behind my double glazed triple bolted door
Central heating on full blast
I watch you glide past
In just a t-shirt and shorts

Indeed
It is me who is cold.

SUNDAY ISLES

What's this feeling inside that leads me to the sound of my own breath?

Here we are
Daily now
Walking the Sunday isles

Is there anybody here left or just bodies?
Hardly a decent question but suitable and telling.

PASSING THROUGH

Little was the drag that Russian heart evoked
Let me help you with your bags are you going home?
By train, five minutes from here, my strength had truly hoped

One bag from six my arm allowed
One word from one left his Russian mouth
"Bus"

On the other side of town

Three steps ahead he quickly led as I heard the train go by
With pace applied no glimpse behind five bags would him suffice
So warming a heart that Russian had for his home built on ice

I felt my strength start to rise from a fire deep inside
A heart that once ate from shallow bags was once again alive
The depth that Russian fire touched would rap me till I die
One pace ahead I led the way until we said goodbye.

THE ALTRUIST

Altruism yells out despise self-interest
Living for others through the mask of modesty
Wouldn't last five minutes in the lions den
Telling how sacrifice turns boys into men

Altruistic sperm not following natures law
As if the whole of creation was a ridiculous flaw
Choosing stagnation death that never lived
Non-existence voted in as our daily call

Okay let's say the altruist did last five minutes in the den
Half eaten and scared witless with his body now shared
Back home gaining reputation by spreading his advantageous glory
Writing a number one best seller *The Hypocrite's Story*

Like a Beatles a Presley a Monet or Warhol
A copy now finds itself in every household
It's simply time that makes stuff traditional
Familiarity, feet up, are we feeling comfortable?

But the lions are still hungry and come knocking on his door
This time nature is ready to settle up an old score
First a warm up by watching Day Of The Dead
And when the film's over they'll take their daily bread

But with reputation on the line the altruist isn't ready for defeat
Screaming we'll take this to the people it's there we will meet
So nature calmly shook hands with the slime of pretence
Loving a story full of suspense

The scene was set the stadium full
Microphone in hand announcing to all
I sacrifice my life my body my soul
Burn me alive till I'm as black as the coal

But sacrifice means there is something to lose and nothing to gain
Do not the selfish end up simply pointing the finger of blame?

Then I shall only give for now I am naught
So you can live on thus let it be taught

Then let naught be taught in every school
Rip up every book so we can all play the fool

But this is not the end to the story of hypocrisy
With so many readers hanging on to words of absurdity
Not yet have you realised the stakes involved
Until true altruism is expressed it is left unresolved

So the naught peace, understanding and life you imply
Will not be denied
Murder will spread to every corner of the globe
Your kingdom filling seven billion hearts with dread
And you will be recognised for all you have said

On a thrown you will sit admired by all
STOP! you will demand, for I am but small
So your words will be granted and written into law
And out of your kingdom you will eternally fall.

THE BREEZE

Warning, maximum penalty one thousand pounds
Expressed in the familiar red white and black
Spring has come early whistles the breeze
From behind a locked window still singing with ease

Over my shoulder lie the wounded fields
With the sprawl of the city slicing through daffodils
Red number 7 and white number 2
Neighbours who've never said how do you do

Air balloon drifting high up above
Black and yellow stripes like a giant bumble bee
Back in the wound in concrete cages we built
Children kicking a ball too young to know guilt

On the edge of the wound looking beyond
There's a fearless doe who ain't gonna be conned
Deep in her pocket she grabs the keys
Unlocks the window and frees the breeze.

LEVELLING

The tornado stirs at will
Coming out of the mist like a ghost
A chilling twist in the dragon's tail
Ripping apart wishful rainbows

The artist's brush filled with creative desperation
The unknowing application of destiny
Fear existing only in the stare of anticipation
Like petrified flies that dream of the spider's architectural ability

We are all architects as we take our first breath
As we watch tangled sugar shocked empires nervously hoping
Dreaming of pots of gold at the roulette wheel
While the tornado plays house at casinos

A flimsy "Do Not Disturb" sign won't keep us snug for eternity
As the arrival of a tornado breaks any deep sleep
For birth, death and tornadoes don't separate or hibernate
They share themselves in the universal exhibition of creativity.

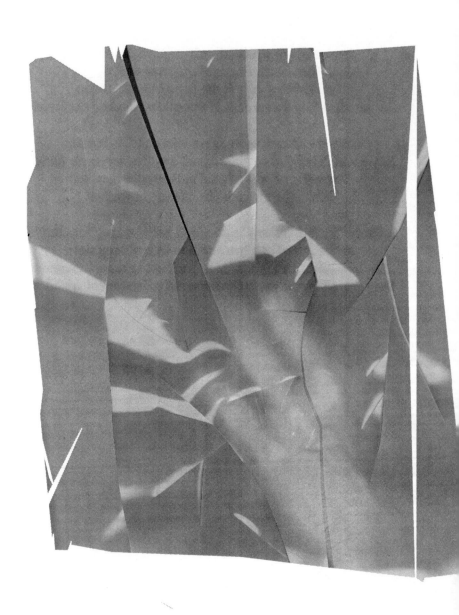

THE ARGUMENT

That feeling of insanity rising up inside
Disorientation and isolation ready to collide
All the love disappears in a puff of smoke
Shaking behind my prison walls as I start to choke

Cascading down the rabbit hole the sunlight quickly fades
Deep inside my history on which my bed is made
Digging through the layers that turn my heart to coal
Hunting down the vermin that's feeding on my soul

Words slice through the thickest skin blood already spilled
Seven thousand children slaughtered on the battle field
As hell unfolds in front of me I fall to my knees
Feeling kind of sleepy my panic starts to ease

You have had enough a voice then softly said
Get up on your feet and rise up from the dead
There is nothing to forgive now understanding you have chose
As the breath of sunlight touched my cheek
I started playing with my toes.

SACRIFICE 1
DEBT

A warning announcing to treasure free time
For when your treasure is born
It is time you will mourn
When a parent is full of regret
A baby is born in debt.

SACRIFICE 2
DROP BY DROP

My only son is to be used as a mop
Washing away blood with blood
Sparing not a drop
His every pore will bleed
To nourish the seed
And you will all follow
Drop by drop.

SACRIFICE 3
EVERY WORD

I have much more important things to do than to be here with you
But I'll give you the time of the day
Uninterested I am in every word that you say
But I swear I won't go astray.

IF

If I knew I would get two cups of water by throwing one away
I would never thirst
If I knew there was a beautiful life after death
Dying would be but a sweet transition

I would not fear gamble lie or deceive
Prey or beg down on my knees
I would not compromise despise or suppress
No more walking around in a guise of fancy dress

I'd need no contracts to make us follow lawless rules
In a casino of distrust for lifeless fools
I'd need no forgiveness for the things that I do
As if being human was the eternal taboo

With responsibility awareness and empathy
I would start writing my testimony
These three things would be my only guide
For then I would have nothing to hide

If I knew
If I only knew.

FOOLS GOLD

The twist can only twist at the end
For right now there is little to bend
So later old buddy with hands open wide
These words will fall to your side

Maybe you're at a slight disadvantage
To someone who's been here before
As I play you this song and pull you along
To the rhythm of the conquistador

You've built up your wall of defence
On a foundation of wisdom immense
So I'll visit your boarders and act under orders
In a world of game show pretence

With barbaric words chosen carefully
A scripted dance I present before you
Scribbling wiggling hips are wetting your lips
You reach out for the taboo.

Trophies reflecting your life in detail
Giving meaning to every stage
Such revenge for the years of repression
Expressing your land of the brave

But the tear shows there is nowhere to hide
A smudged mask exposing the lie
Shadows of doubt start crawling about
Alone again with your burnt fantasy pie

I know how much you adore
The pictures I've painted for you
But it's time old buddy with hands open wide
To let these words fall to my side.

CONCRETE CORNER

Born in concrete corner
Cross bones flying high
A memory of rushing water
Flapping in the sky

Six inches ahead short sighted I see
Staring at a yellow flower painted just for me
Tattooed in cement like modern day Pompeii
Soon will come the rapids to wash it all away.

LILY THE PINK

There's a pinky thingy sitting in the river
Throw some thingy in and save its lily life
Doesn't seem distressed ain't no bubbles rising
It's anchored down you clown where's my thingy knife.

DON'T MISS THE NEXT BIG FREEDOM

When freedom is a simple genre written in a book
A piece of luxury literature for the well fed
A standing ovation in a concert hall
It becomes the unknown soldier born to be dead

When freedom is the present hero who's taking all the votes
A state of moderate desperation rallying passive hopes
A moan about corruption that makes only some of us look clean
A nice idea for a little while when buzzing off caffeine

Then freedom is nothing more than half desires we will call regrets
A hand full of well rehearsed apologies for not winning the bets
A bunch of autumn if onlys I could live it all again
A thank your lucky stars you still have the freedom to complain.

THIS JOURNEY

Like a word which has made itself at home on the tip of my tongue
This journey's never quite spoken.

LIFE LINE

There's this river you see
Flowing just for me
Gonna go there today
Got this feeling it'll wash me away

What's that lying on its bed?
Winding its way like a thread
It's telling to even think that cats could die
Just because they like to see what's inside.

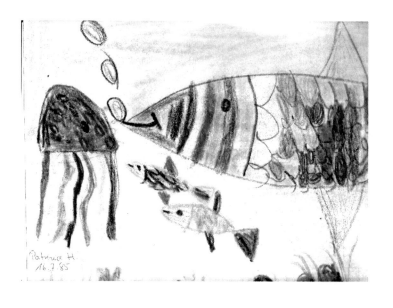

THE BREATH OF DEBT

You told me I'm a sinner before asking me my name
Gave me a national insurance number to point out who's to blame
You said I have to earn a living I have to earn to live
My birth life and death to the system I must give

What do you want to be when you grow up, as if I had a choice
Before I could answer with *me* to declare I had a voice
You turned me into a trainee to follow in your shoes
As you poured this baby a glass of your second-fiddle booze

Get this down you kid for this is how it's gonna be
For what you are about to receive that's your history
You can thank the ones above for pulling all the strings
And you will call them Gov' King of all your kings

Don't forget now child people died so you could live
Sacrifice the spice of life the only way to give
So be on your guard cos life is hard nothing is for free
It's written in the book The Vatican Apple Tree.

THE BUTTERFLY OF SPRING

Life is like a conveyor belt full of thoughts passing by
So lay beside me in the field and watch the clouds in the sky
So tender is the touch, that warming breeze upon my cheek
Through the butterfly of spring life once again starts to speak

But now I see a big red stop sign so real in front of my eyes
Screaming out obsessively the clouds are in disguise
They're impersonators of truth turning reason into obscenity
It's order and control we need to tame this vicious calamity

A flock of birds take off at the sound of gnashing teeth
As a squad of empty hearts drum to the wild beast
Like expressionless machines they level out the land
Till the sap flows from the dying tree and the water turns to sand

Now fighting to survive I start grabbing all I can
Turning boys into cannon fodder at the sight of Uncle Sam
My grip obsessively tightens around a hollow anchor
As a crazed stare turns the clouds into a fading blur

So now I have a reason, be it to die for nothing
Other than the idea that butterflies are disgusting
So I chain up my stake, my pride, my land
And hang out a sign that clearly demands
Trespassers will be prosecuted!!!
That's the law, that's the command

My mind now numb to the beat of the drum
I welcome in the winter
To hibernate and rest from hate
Leaving behind a heart trained to be a splinter

And so I'll sleep ten thousand years dreaming of the spring
Lying in the field of peace the trees once again start to sing

You see, it's not the pain that hurts but the fear of being hurt
So I filled my life with fear and slowly found comfort in the dirt
Just following orders, humanity's home made straight jacket
Flicking through my life once again I heard that beastly racket

A flock of birds take off at the sound of gnashing teeth
But as that familiar bang broke my sleep, I now felt their loving wreath
So now I fly with the clouds in the sky for no longer am I meek
For only through the butterfly of spring life really starts to speak.

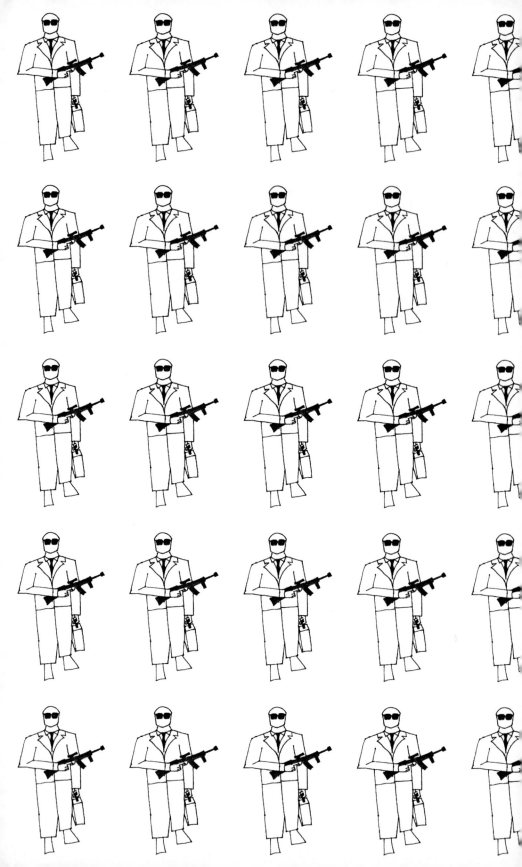

THE APPLE TREE

A deep hole was dug when planting my seed
Ten thousand years of darkness I'd bleed
Then breaking the surface I breathed my first breath
And felt the warm sun and the knowledge of death

Here I can see the seasons come and go
Hear the birds singing how the river does flow
Listen to the trees with the wind deep in their leaves
Discovering friendships with a natural ease

I became a new home for the singers of love
As I lived my life from the heart of a dove
Then out of the blue I was told to follow the word
From a far away source who made itself heard

Here you were born this is your name
Sign your mark here it's no longer a game
Cover that flesh have you no shame
You'll end up in jail with only yourself to blame

Confusion I felt, what had I done wrong?
Listening to the birds singing the river song?
So many questions from such a weak lung
Here are the answers now hold your tongue

The source had suddenly spoken to me
Told me what I am and pronounced me guilty
With fear in my heart I threw away the dove
Ready to die for the land I now love

I'm a wild animal you see from out of the trees
The whip of the tamer has me down on my knees
Jumping through razor sharp hoops to earn my next feed
Ten thousand years of darkness my skin did it bleed

The crowd roared at the skill of the tamer's whip
Under lock and key the rule book strapped to his hip
Puzzling the mind with cheap phantasmagoria
Life became a second rate store of plastic memorabilia

My few minutes of fame playing the game
Had come to an end for now I was lame
My strength had all gone back to the river
So the whip turned to the crowd growling now you will deliver

Yes the hole was deep so deep we slept
Ten thousand years the tamer and I had wept
So now we declare that the river really does flow
As we walk hand in hand up the apple tree we go

The chain of despair then started to loosen its grip
As the word of the source fell away from the hip
Breaking the surface we now breathe our next breath
And feel the warm sun dissolve the illusion of death.

EQUALITY

Equality needs no colour code
It doesn't encourage cooking on a plastic stove
Pointing the hypocritical finger of blame
At history only when we suddenly feel the shame

It's not an ethnic questionnaire ticking this box if you are fair
Balancing colours while painting by numbers
Trendy political correctness to tone down the glare
Trying to disguise the truthful stare

Equality isn't some decorated phoney liberalism
Fancy tonal patchwork giving the impression of progression
A self deceiving glance that has to convince itself it's colour blind
Acting like some enlightened duster
That thinks it can suddenly sweep away a mucky past

It's not about going out of our way to smile at other colours
Fearing the depth of our own rabbit hole of prejudice
By *trying* to be sisters and brothers
Trying must stop before anything can be achieved
Like trying to breathe and hoping to believe.

COMPROMISE

Agreeing on something we disagree with
Do we disagree with living should we compromise on that?
Maybe cut down on breathing
Tell our lungs that we are leaving
On the next train to asbestos
Where the blood is always spat?

Like a peace treaty that is signed only to run out
A glossy short sighted drunken handshake for the camera
The front page headline now reading *AT LEAST WE TRIED!!!*
As life becomes a quick fix façade of Class A ephemera

CNN with *Your World Today*
Commercial break we'll be right back
Don't go away come what may
Religiously providing answers at the drop of a hat

These are the rules and these are the tools
Religion, military and the monetary system
A three fold engine with its ridged drive
Paradoxically forcing its cogs to bend and hide

So keep sweeping the dirt under the carpet
Hoping a magical vacuum will suck it all away
Talk about deep oceans while only wetting the ankles
As we head for a black hole busy reading
THE QUEEN IS NOW OFFICIALLY GAY!!!

Distrusting our ability to find concrete resolution
We take all the mirrors down rejecting naked truth
Back to the wall sensing resignation
Anything for a quiet life we start living out the spoof

Half interested, half empty, isolated and misunderstood
Still strangers after 50 years asking:
Who is this in front of me?
Get the morning paper headline *THE WORLD IN DEBT!!!*
As history repeats itself like a scratched vinyl called Regret

50% off officially qualifies us as civilised
Left leans right, right leans left, fascists in the middle
With humanity diagnosed as selfish wild regression
Compromise becomes law our saviour and the meaning of
progression.

Michael Victor Jackson